WHAT'S YOUR VIEWPOINT?

TERRORISM

ARE WE ALL AT RISK?

Anita Croy

LUCENT PRESS

Published in 2020 by
Lucent Press, an Imprint of Greenhaven Publishing, LLC
353 3rd Avenue
Suite 255
New York, NY 10010

Copyright © 2020 Lucent Press, an Imprint of Greenhaven Publishing, LLC.

All rights reserved. No part of this book may be reproduced in any form without permission in writing from the publisher, except by a reviewer.

Produced for Lucent by Calcium
Editors: Sarah Eason and Tim Cooke
Designers: Paul Myerscough and Lynne Lennon
Picture researcher: Rachel Blount

Picture credits: Cover: Shutterstock: Arindambanerjee (fg), Fishman64 (bg). Inside: Shutterstock: David Ortega Baglietto: p. 15; Orhan Cam: p. 22; Cosimoattanasio – Redline: p. 18; Chris DeRidder and Hans VandenNieuwendijk: p. 33; Fishman64: p. 1; Ben Gingell: p. 35; John Gomez: p. 21; Jerome460: p. 23; Jstone: p. 19; Thomas Koch: p. 24; Lia Koltyrina: p. 28; Greg Kushmerek: p. 34; Alexandros Michailidis: p. 43; Pogorelova Olga: p. 41; Orlok: p. 13; Prazis Images: p. 10; Railway fx: p. 17; Rawpixel.com: p. 20; Alexandre Rotenberg: p. 42; TADAphotographer: p. 14; Ken Tannenbaum: p. 7; Tero Vesalainen: p. 4; View Apart: p. 30; Leonard Zhukovsky: p. 29; Wikimedia Commons: Aude: p. 25; Mahmoud Bali (VOA): p. 16; Navy Petty Officer 1st Class Michael Billings: p. 32; Cal Sr from Newport, NC, US: p. 36; Flibirigit: p. 40; Mike Herbst from Berlin, Germany: p. 27; High Contrast: p. 8; Staff Sergeant Mark A. More: p. 9; Tim Pierce: p. 37; Queerbubbles: p. 39; RekonDog: p. 26; TSGT Cedric H. Rudisill, USAF: p. 6; Sitomon: p. 11; T.B.H. Stenhouse: p. 38; Pete Souza, White House: p. 12; U.S. Navy photo by Chief Mass Communication Specialist Bill Mesta: p. 31.

Cataloging-in-Publication Data

Names: Croy, Anita.
Title: Terrorism: Are We All At Risk? / Anita Croy.
Description: New York : Lucent Press, 2020. | Series: What's your viewpoint?
| Includes glossary and index.
Identifiers: ISBN 9781534565753 (pbk.) | ISBN 9781534565760 (library bound)
| ISBN 9781534565777 (ebook)
Subjects: LCSH: Terrorism--Juvenile literature.
Classification: LCC HV6431.C79 2020 | DDC 363.325--dc23

Printed in the United States of America

CPSIA compliance information: Batch #BS19KL: For further information contact Greenhaven Publishing LLC, New York, New York at 1-844-317-7404.

Please visit our website, www.greenhavenpublishing.com. For a free color catalog of all our high-quality books, call toll free 1-844-317-7404 or fax 1-844-317-7405.

Contents

WHAT'S THE DEBATE?   4

CHAPTER ONE
TERRORISM   6

CHAPTER TWO
MILITANT ISLAMIST TERRORISM   12

CHAPTER THREE
PREVENTING TERRORISM   18

CHAPTER FOUR
SURVEILLANCE AND PRIVACY   24

CHAPTER FIVE
TREATMENT OF TERRORISTS   30

CHAPTER SIX
DOMESTIC TERRORISM   36

TERRORISM: WHAT'S NEXT?   42

THE FUTURE: WHAT'S YOUR VIEWPOINT?   44

Glossary   46

For More Information   47

Index   48

TERRORISM

What's the Debate?

Terrorism is the use of indiscriminate violence to spread fear among large numbers of people. It is often carried out by small groups to try to achieve political, religious, or social change. There are many types of terrorist attacks, but most target unarmed civilians. They might take the form of bombings, mass shootings, stabbings, taking and killing hostages, or seizing means of transportation, such as aircraft. Terrorists sometimes justify the harm they inflict by arguing that their cause is more important than the fate of individuals. For most people, however, terrorism is not an acceptable way to try to achieve any kind of political or religious ends.

This book looks at the debates surrounding international and domestic terrorism. Read each chapter to find out about one debate. Then examine the ✓ and ✗ features at the end of the chapter, which explain both sides of the debate. Finally, review the "What's Your Viewpoint?" feature at the end of the chapter to make up your own mind about the debate. You can also find out what viewpoint people in leading positions hold by reading the "What's Their Viewpoint?" features. Let's start by taking a look at two arguments about how much of a threat terrorism is.

Terrorists want people to see threats everywhere, to try to disrupt their everyday lives.

WHAT'S THE DEBATE?

DEBATING TERRORISM

TERRORISM IS A SERIOUS THREAT

- There have been seven major terrorist attacks in the United States since 2000, with many deaths. Any major attack could cause dozens or hundreds of deaths.

- Terrorists can strike anywhere. There are so many possible targets that it is impossible to protect them all.

- Many Islamist extremists dislike the United States, because of its involvement in the politics of some Muslim countries.

- Terrorists within the United States have easy access to guns and other weapons to carry out attacks.

TERRORISM IS NOT A SERIOUS THREAT

- Terrorism is intended by terrorists to seem to be more of a threat than it really is. The number of victims is very small compared to the size of the population of the United States.

- The intelligence agencies often disrupt terror plots before they are carried out.

- The number of terrorist attacks is falling around the world.

- Many of the governments and other groups that back terrorists have been destroyed or weakened.

TERRORISM

CHAPTER ONE
TERRORISM

Terrorism has existed for centuries. In its modern meaning of indiscriminate attacks on the general public, it became more common in the second half of the 1900s. These attacks are usually directed at "soft targets," which means they are undefended and have no reason to be targeted. Such attacks enable tiny groups of terrorists to shock millions of people to try to change their behavior or to call attention to a cause. Placing a bomb in a crowded shopping mall or sending deadly chemicals in the mail spreads fear that anyone might become the victim of a random attack. The idea behind terrorism is that if enough people become very frightened, they will demand that the government act to protect them. They might urge their government to give in to the terrorists' demands. However, there are few examples in history of this policy actually succeeding. More often, terrorist groups end in failure. They are destroyed by security forces, split up, or fade away without achieving their aims.

On 9/11/2001, terrorists flew a passenger airliner into the Pentagon in Washington, D.C.

A Different Kind of Terrorism

Another type of terrorism has vague aims. Attacks in the United States and Canada have been carried out by young men who identify themselves as incels, for example. Incel is short for "involuntary celibate," which refers to a young man who is angry about being single.

Incels blame women for their lack of success in relationships. In some cases, they have turned to violence. In October 2015, for example, an incel shot nine people dead in Roseburg, Oregon. Like other terrorists, incels are ready to die during their attacks. They leave messages justifying their actions. However, such attacks have no purpose other than to express the rage and frustration of the perpetrators (people who carry out attacks). No change in government policy will make it easier for young men to get along better with young women.

One of the Twin Towers of the World Trade Center in New York City burns after the attacks of 9/11.

International and Domestic Terrorism

Incels are one of the groups behind domestic terrorist attacks within the United States. These are attacks carried out by US citizens against other Americans within their own country. International terrorism is defined as attacks carried out by citizens of another country against Americans, either within the United States or abroad. Another phrase, "homegrown terrorism," is often used to describe attacks that are carried out by US citizens whose motivation is more international. This might include, for example, American Islamists who carry out attacks in support of an extremist form of Islam. They learn about extremism from the Middle East, where it is more common.

TERRORISM

History of Terrorism

The modern history of terrorism began in the 1970s. Small groups around the world tried to bring about change. In the Middle East, for example, the Palestine Liberation Organization (PLO) began a terrorist campaign against Israel. They believed Israel had occupied land that belonged to the Palestinians. They saw terrorism as a way they could advance their cause against Israel and its supporters, which included the United States.

This memorial lists the members of the Israeli team killed by Palestinian terrorists at the Munich Olympics in 1972.

In Europe, meanwhile, terrorists tried to achieve independence. The Irish Republican Army (IRA) was set up by Catholics in southern Ireland. Northern Ireland is part of the United Kingdom, and about half of its population is Protestant. The IRA wanted it to become part of the Republic of Ireland, which is mainly Catholic. A period of violence known as the Troubles lasted from the late 1960s until 1998 when a peace agreement was signed. More than 3,500 people died.

Domestic Terrorism

In the United States, organizations such as the Weathermen carried out terrorist attacks in the 1970s. They were protesting US wars overseas. In 1995, an attack led by Timothy McVeigh blew up a federal building in Oklahoma City, killing 168 people. The attack was motivated by the terrorists' hatred of the government. They accused it of attacking individuals' freedom.

TERRORISM

WHAT'S THEIR VIEWPOINT?

Daniel L. Byman is a senior fellow at the Center for Middle East Policy. In December 2017, he wrote a review of the year for the Brookings Institution in which he celebrated the successes of counterterrorism. Counterterrorism is the efforts of intelligence agencies to stop terrorist attacks before they happen. Byman wrote that, in order to keep protecting the public from terrorism, US lawmakers should focus on trying to find solutions to wars and unrest in the Middle East and should look at the rise of white, right-wing violence within America. Agencies should also focus on responses to methods of terrorist attack, such as ramming with vehicles.

Attacks of 9/11

The most well-known terrorist attack of recent times came on 9/11, 2001. Militant Islamists seized four airliners and crashed them into the World Trade Center in New York City and the Pentagon in Washington, D.C. One aircraft crashed in Pennsylvania after passengers fought with the terrorists. Soon after the towers of the World Trade Center were attacked, they both collapsed. About 3,000 people died, including 19 terrorists. The attack shocked the world. It was soon traced to a group called al-Qaeda, which supports a radical form of Islam.

First responders search for survivors in the wreckage of the Oklahoma City bombing.

9

Spreading Fear

Between 2006 and 2016, according to one estimate, nearly 217,000 people died in about 127,000 terrorist incidents around the world. The majority died in the Middle East and North Africa. Europe and North America had far fewer victims.

In a poll in 2017, 43 percent of Americans said they were afraid or very afraid of terrorism. In fact, there is statistically very little chance of Americans being involved in a terror attack. These attacks, however, are intended to spread fear, so it is easy to overestimate the threat they represent. For this reason, terrorists often attack famous buildings or targets that are important to many people. Terrorists want to create a feeling that people could be attacked anywhere, at any moment. They aim to terrify as many people as they can.

Some people believe terrorism is justified. They see it as one way a small group of people can make a powerful point. For these supporters, political struggles are too important to worry about a small loss of life. Most people, however, argue that terrorism is just like any other form of indiscriminate murder.

Terrorists set out to make people feel as though they are everywhere. That way, people's fear of an attack is greater than the actual danger.

✓ TERRORISM CAN BE JUSTIFIED

Igor Primoratz is a professor of philosophy at the Hebrew University in Jerusalem, Israel. In April 2013, he wrote a blog about whether terrorism can ever be justified. He wrote that terrorism is wrong because it is utterly unjust and violates human rights. However, Primoratz wrote, when a community faces terrible injustice or danger, it may find terrorism to be "morally permissible," which means it is acceptable.

✗ TERRORISM IS NEVER JUSTIFIED

In 2016, after terrorist attacks in the North African country of Tunisia, human rights organizations in the country wrote a joint letter to their fellow Tunisians. "We strongly affirm that terrorism is an awful crime that can never be excused or justified. It poses a major threat to human rights, beginning with the most fundamental of rights, the right to life. Combating terrorism is a crucial government responsibility."

WHAT'S YOUR VIEWPOINT?

Do you agree with Igor Primoratz's viewpoint, or that of the Tunisian human rights organizations? Use the prompts below to help form your viewpoint.

- Primoratz says that terrorism might be morally acceptable in a situation of grave danger. Who gets to decide when danger justifies terrorism?
- The Tunisians call the right to life the most basic of all rights. If the death penalty is acceptable, however, does that also mean terrorism is?
- The Tunisians say it is government's job to combat terrorism. Who else could do this?

Terrorists can be heroes in some communities. This painting celebrates terrorists in Northern Ireland.

TERRORISM

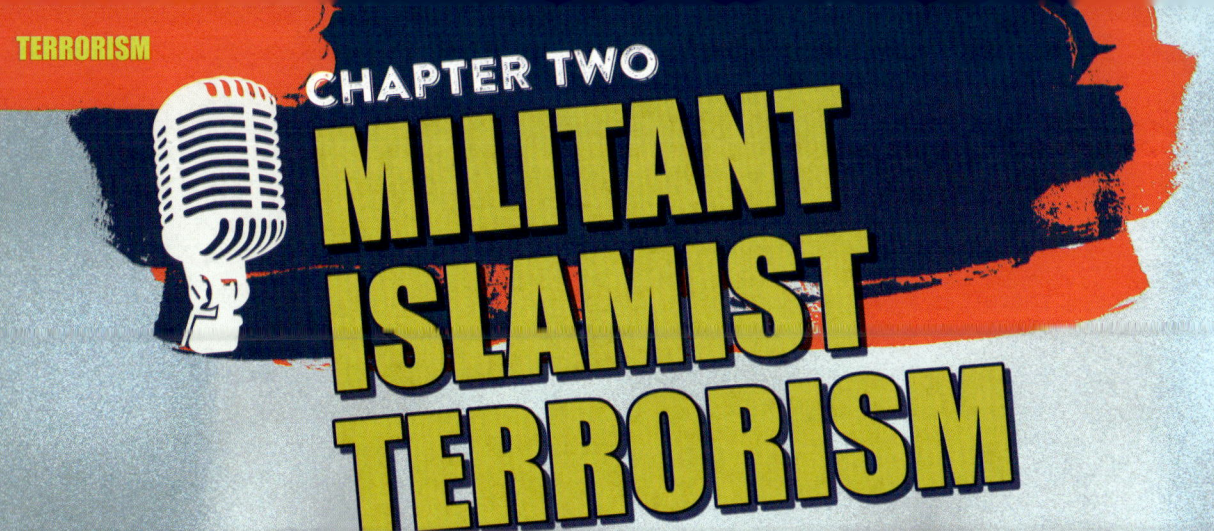

CHAPTER TWO
MILITANT ISLAMIST TERRORISM

One of the highest-profile types of international terrorism is militant Islamist terrorism. It is carried out by Muslim groups that want to enforce a very strict form of Islam. There are various groups in different parts of the world. In Afghanistan, for example, the Taliban launches attacks against the government. The Afghan government is supported by the United States and other Western countries. In Pakistan, Taliban members opposed to female education shot and nearly killed the schoolgirl Malala Yousafzai in 2012. After she recovered, she became a leading international figure supporting female education worldwide.

In Israel, Hamas carries out terrorist attacks against Jewish citizens as part of a long campaign against Israel. In Syria, where a civil war began in 2011, the Islamic State in Iraq and Syria (ISIS) used terrorist tactics to seize land it intended to use to form the basis of a caliphate—a religious state that would eventually cover most of the Middle East. In early 2019, ISIS remained active not only in Iraq and Syria but also in Libya.

Malala Yousafzai (center) meets Barack and Michelle Obama. Malala became a campaigner for girls' rights.

MILITANT ISLAMIST TERRORISM

US aircraft often drop bombs on Islamic State positions in Syria.

Militant Islamism and the West

Militant Islamist terrorism mainly affects Islamic countries. There are two main branches of Islam. Sunni and Shia terrorists each attack followers of the other group. Terrorists carry out attacks not only in the Middle East, but also in countries such as India and Indonesia. Militant Islamist terrorists have also launched attacks on targets in Europe and North America. Some Muslims believe Islam is "at war" with Western values. Some radical imams, or preachers, reject the freedoms enjoyed in the West and in parts of the Middle East and other Muslim-majority countries. For example, they say everyone must dress according to their strict interpretations of the rules of the Islamic holy book, the Koran.

In addition, many Muslims—not just extremists—resent the West's history of interfering in the Islamic world. In the 1800s and 1900s, European nations and the United States took control of parts of Asia, North Africa, and the Middle East for political and economic reasons. One of the economic reasons was that these regions had large supplies of oil. Western countries set up colonies or backed governments to get access to the valuable oil.

Today, interference in the Muslim world continues. The United States, for example, sent troops to fight in Syria when the civil war broke out. This interference in the Muslim world has led to a mistrust and resentment of the West on the part of some Muslims, which has, in turn, led to an increase in Islamist extremism.

TERRORISM

Islam and Violence

The number of terrorist attacks carried out by Muslims sometimes seems much higher than those carried out by people of other faiths. In addition, some militant Islamists claim terrorism is supported by Islamic teaching. Suicide bombers blow themselves up believing they will go straight to paradise. To some observers in the West, this gives the impression that Islam approves of violence and murder.

Most Islamic scholars agree that there is nothing in the Koran that supports terrorism.

The nature of Islam's relation to violence has been widely studied. Islamic scholars and others are trying to understand the apparent hatred of the West among a small number of Muslims. Some imams in the United Kingdom and Europe, for example, have called upon their fellow Muslims to launch attacks against the societies among which they live. Most Muslims reject such calls.

Hate preaching is illegal virtually everywhere. Many preachers who promote violence have been sent to jail. Mosques have been closed down if they were suspected of trying to convince worshipers to adopt a violent form of Islam. The majority of Muslims and community organizations widely criticize the actions of dangerous radicals. However, the fact that preachers are encouraging terrorist attacks seems to some observers to underline the association between Islam and violence.

MILITANT ISLAMIST TERRORISM

The Role of Jihad

One of the central ideas in Islamist terrorism is jihad. Today, the phrase is most often translated as meaning "holy war." It is taken to describe a conflict between Islam and Christianity. In many ways, it is seen as a continuation of centuries of conflict. The religions began to fight in the 1000s, when European Christians launched the first of a series of crusades to take control of the Holy Land from the Muslims who lived there. In this interpretation of jihad, Muslims are encouraged to kill unbelievers, or non-Muslims. Muslims who die in this struggle are rewarded after death in Paradise.

Many Muslim scholars, however, argue that the idea of jihad does not refer to a war between religions. Instead, it refers to a personal struggle to keep one's faith in the face of doubt. In this interpretation, jihad is an internal, spiritual conflict. It has nothing to do with physical violence. The vast majority of Muslims see Islam as a peaceful religion built upon ideas of respect, duty, and looking after others. They reject any idea that it promotes violence or that it does not value non-Muslim life.

Many Muslims point out that a Muslim is no more likely to be a terrorist than anyone else.

WHAT'S THEIR VIEWPOINT?

Daniel L. Byman is an expert on the Middle East. In December 2017, he noted that the threat of international Islamist terrorism had fallen because of the defeat of terror groups such as ISIS. He saw that in terrorist attacks in the West the attacker was now likely to say that they carried out the attack in the name of ISIS, but were no longer directly instructed by them. Such attackers were usually less dangerous than attackers trained by terrorist groups.

TERRORISM

Radical Islam

There are two main branches of Islam, Shia and Sunni, but there are many schools of Muslim thought. They are all based on the teachings of the Prophet Muhammad, as recorded in the Koran in the 600s. Most scholars and ordinary Muslims agree that Islam is a religion of peace. It justifies violence only in self-defense.

Some Muslims believe the Koran should be interpreted strictly. They reject laws that are not based on Islamic teachings. Groups such as the Taliban in Afghanistan and Pakistan, the Muslim Brotherhood in Egypt, and ISIS in Syria and Iraq, want to establish strict Islamist governments. They believe the Koran justifies attacks on non-Muslims to achieve this goal.

Radical Islamist groups are banned in many Western countries. However, they use the Internet to spread propaganda designed to make Muslims angry with how Western powers treat other Muslims. It encourages Muslims to develop more radical views. Some of these individuals have launched attacks on behalf of terrorist groups they have only been in contact with via the Internet.

Fighting and destruction in Syrian cities such as Raqqa encourage extremists to blame the West.

MILITANT ISLAMIST TERRORISM

✓ ISLAM IS A RELIGION OF VIOLENCE

Abu Bakr al-Baghdadi, leader of ISIS, released this message about Islam in 2015. "Islam was never a religion of peace. Islam is the religion of fighting. No one should believe that the war that we are waging is the war of the Islamic State. It is the war of all Muslims, but the Islamic State is spearheading [leading] it. It is the war of Muslims against infidels [non-Muslims]. Oh Muslims, go to war everywhere. It is the duty of every Muslim."

✗ ISLAM IS NOT A VIOLENT RELIGION

Hazrat Mirza Masroor Ahmad is the world head of the Ahmadiyya group of Muslims. At a speech in London in 2016, he said that Islam totally forbids suicide, so suicide attacks and all other forms of terrorism are against Islamic teaching. The only war ever permitted by Islamic teaching would be a war forced by self-defense.

WHAT'S YOUR VIEWPOINT?

These two leaders of Islamic groups have very different views of Islam. Consider these points to see which view you most agree with.

- Opinion polls show that most Muslims reject terrorism. Why do you think al-Baghdadi might claim that ISIS is fighting for all Muslims?
- Masroor Ahmad says that Islam permits Muslims to fight a defensive war. Is that different from what Christian teachings say?
- If Islam forbids suicide, why might suicide bombers believe that their actions can be justified?

ISIS wants to fly its flag in the Middle East, over a caliphate governed by a strict form of Islam.

17

TERRORISM

CHAPTER THREE
PREVENTING TERRORISM

There is little doubt that a small number of Muslims have a great suspicion of the West and its values and culture. They also resent the international influence of the United States and Europe. Militant Islamist terrorists have carried out attacks in North America and in European cities such as Paris and London.

Militant Islamist attacks in the United States have been carried out both by foreign terrorists and by Muslims who were born and raised as Americans. Most Americans cannot understand why anyone would be so aggressive toward their neighbors. Some homegrown terrorists are inspired by the Internet. They watch radical propaganda that claims US forces are treating Muslims badly in the Middle East. Other American Muslim terrorists are inspired by the politics of their family homelands, or by US support for Israel.

Islamist Attack

In December 2015, terrorists attacked a workplace party in San Bernardino, California. They killed 14 people and seriously injured 22 more.

In the West, many people associate terrorism almost completely with Islam.

PREVENTING TERRORISM

The terrorists were Pakistani-born Tashfeen Malik, who was a legal permanent resident of the United States, and her husband, Syed Rizwan Farook, a US citizen of Pakistani descent. The pair carried out the attack in the name of a radical form of Islam.

At the time of the San Bernardino attack, Donald Trump was campaigning to become the Republican candidate for president. After the attack, he called for a ban on Muslims entering the United States while US intelligence figured out how to screen Muslims entering the country. Trump said, "Those who do not believe in our Constitution, or who support bigotry and hatred, will not be admitted for immigration into the country."

Before he became US president, Donald Trump had a history of blaming Muslims for terror attacks.

A Ban Is Introduced

After Trump became president in January 2017, one of his earliest actions was to sign Executive Order 13769. It banned Muslim immigrants from seven countries—Iran, Iraq, Libya, Somalia, Sudan, Syria, and Yemen—although non-Muslim citizens of those countries were still allowed to enter the United States.

The ban also cut the number of refugees allowed into the United States to 50,000 per year, with none at all from Syria. Trump argued that letting in refugees from Syria might let in supporters of ISIS, who would try to harm Americans. The president's critics said it was people such as those fleeing the fighting in Syria who had most need of refuge in countries such as the United States.

TERRORISM

A Ban on Muslims

There are about 1.8 billion Muslims, one-quarter of the world's population. They include many from countries that are allies of the United States. Experts on foreign relations warned that a ban risked upsetting those countries. It might also reduce cooperation between US intelligence agencies and their colleagues in Muslim countries. This cooperation is vital to learning about international terrorist networks and planned attacks.

About 3.45 million Muslims live in the United States. The majority take part in most aspects of US society.

Executive Order 13769 caused outrage in America and abroad. About 700 travelers were detained as they entered the United States. A further 60,000 visas were suspended, so their holders could not travel to the United States. There were public protests around the country. Lawyers headed to airports to help immigrants get admitted to the United States.

Civil rights organizations went to court to stop the ban. They claimed the ban was unconstitutional, because it discriminated against people on the grounds of their religion alone. Only two months after the ban was introduced, it was suspended so it could be studied by the courts. In response, the White House issued a new executive order. The new order used different language to suggest that this was not a "Muslim ban."

PREVENTING TERRORISM

Trump's proposed ban on Muslim travelers caused protests around the world, including this one in London, UK.

It no longer allowed non-Muslims from the affected countries to enter the United States. It also allowed citizens from those countries to apply for visas. Again, the order was suspended.

In September 2017, President Trump issued a third version of the travel ban. It dropped Sudan from the list of banned countries while adding Chad, North Korea, and Venezuela. Of these, only Chad has a Muslim majority. The ban was again suspended while it was reviewed. Its opponents claimed Donald Trump's record of negative comments about Islam made it clear the ban was still targeting Muslims. The Supreme Court disagreed. It ruled in June 2018 that the ban was indeed constitutional, and the ban went into force at ports and airports.

WHAT'S THEIR VIEWPOINT?

Albert Ford is a program associate at New America, a think tank in Washington, D.C. In August 2017, he noted that the threat from terrorism in the United States comes almost entirely from US citizens. No foreign terrorist group has successfully attacked the country since September 11, 2001. Since then, far more people have been killed by right-wing attacks than by militant Islamist attacks.

21

TERRORISM

Halting Terror

After the US Supreme Court ruled that it was legal, the travel ban went into force in June 2018. However, observers argued that it would do little to halt terrorism inside the United States.

No attacks have been carried out inside the United States by terrorists from any country on the list. The 9/11 attackers, for example, included Saudi Arabians and Egyptians. Some people say that Saudi Arabia and Egypt should have been on the list. However, those countries are key US allies and trade partners in the Middle East and North Africa. Critics say this is why they were excluded. In addition, critics point out that other terror attacks have been carried out by Muslim terrorists who would have been in the United States legally, despite the ban. In addition, many experts fear the ban will keep the countries involved from sharing information with US agencies about terrorist activity. This might make it easier for terrorists to plan an attack.

A final argument against the ban is that it has the wrong target. The most frequent terrorist attacks in the United States are not Islamist at all. They are attacks carried out for domestic reasons.

The US Supreme Court ruled 5–4 that the president had the power to ban mainly Muslim travelers.

PREVENTING TERRORISM

✓ THE BAN WILL REDUCE TERRORISM

Tres Watson is a spokesman for the Republican Party of Kentucky. In January 2017, he commented about the original travel ban, which he said was intended to protect the borders of the United States temporarily, preventing the arrival of immigrants and refugees who might pose a threat. He explained that the countries listed in the ban were facing conflicts with militant Islamists or had governments he believed were sponsors of terrorism.

✗ THERE IS NO REASON FOR THE BAN

In April 2018, former intelligence officials told *CNN* that no citizen of the countries affected by the ban had caused any terrorism-related death in the United States since 1975. They said that the goal of counterterrorism was to track individuals who posed real terrorist threats, not to ban 150 million people from the country.

Many protestors warned against the dangers of Islamophobia, which is a hatred of all Muslims.

WHAT'S YOUR VIEWPOINT?

Do you agree with Tres Watson or the intelligence experts? Use the prompts below to help form your viewpoint.

- Tres Watson says that the ban is a temporary measure. Can you think of any evidence that the current threat to the US justifies this move?
- The intelligence experts say that it is wrong to bar 150 million people to stop a handful of terrorists. How else can Americans be kept safe?
- Watson points out that the ban affects refugees. Why might people fleeing conflict or danger be a threat if they came to the United States?

TERRORISM

CHAPTER FOUR
SURVEILLANCE AND PRIVACY

After the terrorist attacks of 9/11, the US security services took steps to help them disrupt the planning for further attacks. These measures included the surveillance, or monitoring, of US citizens. Some people believe such surveillance breaks people's rights to privacy.

The terrorist attacks of September 11, 2001, shocked Americans. Many wondered why the terrorists had not been caught before they had a chance to carry out the attacks. The terrorists who flew the airliners had been trained at flying schools in the United States, for example. The organization behind the attacks was al-Qaeda, which had previously attacked US targets. An al-Qaeda supporter had bombed the World Trade Center in 1993, killing six people. The group had bombed the warship USS *Cole* in Yemen in 2000. Yet the 9/11 attacks took everyone by surprise.

This Pakistani magazine reported the killing of Osama bin Laden, leader of al-Qaeda, by US forces in 2011.

Intelligence Agencies

Tracking terrorist activity overseas is the task of the Central Intelligence Agency (CIA). Watching domestic terrorists is the job of the Federal Bureau of Investigation (FBI). There are also other

SURVEILLANCE AND PRIVACY

US intelligence organizations, including military intelligence. Before the attacks, both the CIA and FBI had warned that the leader of al-Qaeda, Osama bin Laden, was planning a big attack in the United States. However, the warnings were not specific. They had gotten lost in rivalries between the agencies.

After the 9/11 attacks, the US led an international military force that invaded Afghanistan. The Afghan government was sheltering the leaders of al-Qaeda. Meanwhile, the US government studied the intelligence failings that allowed the attacks to take place. It created a new post, Director of National Security. The director has the role of coordinating the operations of all US intelligence agencies. The director is also the senior intelligence advisor to the US government.

The FBI is based in the J. Edgar Hoover Building in Washington, D.C. The agency was criticized for not sharing information.

The Patriot Act

Another consequence of the 9/11 attacks was the USA Patriot Act. The act was passed at the request of the intelligence agencies. It increased their powers to investigate suspected plots so they could prevent attacks before they took place. For example, the act said that the agencies could detain immigrants for as long as they wanted if they thought the prisoners had information about terrorism. The act also allowed intelligence services to search people's homes or businesses without telling them. It gave the FBI increased powers to search people's phone records, computer history, and business records without permission. The act even made it legal for intelligence agencies to collect information about what books people borrowed from public libraries, in case their reading habits suggested they were supporters of terrorism.

TERRORISM

Being Watched

Some Americans are suspicious of any form of surveillance. Up to 250,000 families may live "off-grid." This means they avoid all contact with authorities such as the government. They do not use the power grid or the US mail. They teach their kids at home rather than send them to school.

For most Americans, it is not realistic to avoid all forms of authority. There are times when Americans need to prove who they are, such as by showing the police a driver's license if they ask to see it.

New York City and other cities are using software that can identify faces to prevent terrorism and crime.

Increasing Surveillance

In general, Americans are subject to more surveillance. For example, there are more than 17,000 security cameras in New York City. The NYPD is introducing facial recognition software than can identify individuals and drivers. Many people are uneasy about such monitoring. They say it allows law enforcement to track individuals who have done nothing wrong. One justification for this monitoring is that it will prevent crime, including terrorism. Critics argue, however, that CCTV has not yet stopped an attack—although it has helped identify perpetrators afterward.

SURVEILLANCE AND PRIVACY

✓ SURVEILLANCE KEEPS US SAFE

Mike Rogers was chairman of the House intelligence committee. In 2015, Rogers justified NSA surveillance to the British newspaper *The Guardian*. He said that if a person called the United States from Syria, it was possible that the caller was recruiting someone into a terrorist group or ordering them to do something. It was therefore important to know who they were talking to and what they were saying.

✗ SURVEILLANCE DOES NOT WORK

In 2015, the American Civil Liberties Union (ACLU) reviewed the effects of the Patriot Act. It reported that, in the decade the government's surveillance program had been running, it had never stopped a terrorist attack or identified a single terrorist suspect.

In most US cities, there are fewer and fewer places where citizens are not on camera for much of the time.

WHAT'S YOUR VIEWPOINT?

Do you agree with Mike Rogers or with the ACLU about surveillance? Use the prompts below to form your viewpoint.

- The ACLU says that mass surveillance had never stopped an act of terrorism. Would it change how you see surveillance if it had?
- Do you agree with Mike Rogers that any phone call from Syria is something to be suspicious about?
- Rogers suggests that calls from Syria might be about terrorism operations. Might it also be people calling to catch up with their friends or families in the United States?

TERRORISM

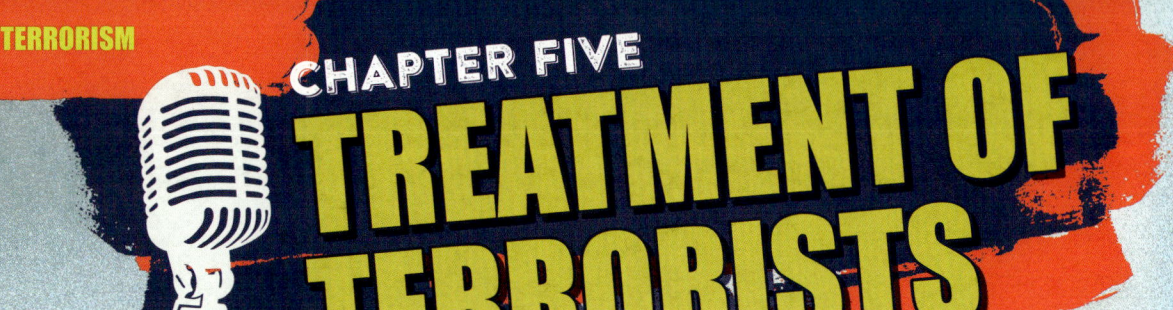

CHAPTER FIVE
TREATMENT OF TERRORISTS

Some experts argue that laws make it more difficult than necessary for law enforcement and intelligence agencies to prevent terrorism. Such agencies have to stick to the law while the people they are trying to catch ignore all normal attitudes toward combat.

In warfare, there are rules about how soldiers should act toward enemy fighters and toward civilians. Terrorists attack unarmed civilians, however. They do not give warnings, and they target people who are not connected to their cause. They often use weapons that kill or wound as many people as possible. However, terrorists are entitled to the same legal rights as any American accused of a crime. They have the right to lawyers and to a fair trial. They are considered innocent until they are found guilty.

Some intelligence agencies and branches of the military have developed new ways of dealing with terrorists. After the 9/11 attacks, for example, some suspected terrorists have been held in detention camps without being charged. They are questioned about any information they have about terrorist activity. However, this is controversial. The US intelligence agencies and military have come under criticism at home and abroad for the way they have treated terrorists or suspected terrorists they have detained.

The US Constitution gives prisoners the right to be free of "cruel and unusual punishments."

30

TREATMENT OF TERRORISTS

The United States leases the base at Guantanamo Bay from Cuba, which still governs the area.

Guantanamo Bay

It is a basic right in US law that no one should be detained without being charged with a crime. There are limits on how long police can detain and question prisoners before they charge them. In 2002, however, the United States set up a prison camp at the Guantanamo Bay US naval base in Cuba. The prison was first known as Camp X-Ray, and later as Camp Delta. The base was used to detain suspected terrorists who had been captured in fighting in Afghanistan after the US-led invasion. Later, detainees were also taken to the camp from other regions of conflict, such as Iraq. These detainees were not charged with specific crimes—they were simply held as prisoners.

People who supported the holding of prisoners without trial pointed out that the inmates at Guantanamo had been detained during combat. They were being held in a military camp. In Cuba, they were beyond the reach of US law. They were therefore not entitled to the same legal process as ordinary Americans. Opponents of the detention said this did not matter. They called for the detainees to be sent to prisons in the United States, where they could have lawyers to represent them. It was important, these people argued, that justice should be seen being done.

TERRORISM

Breaking the Rules?

The way in which US personnel treated captured Muslims from Afghanistan, Iraq, and other conflicts, has been widely criticized. Many Americans objected to the methods used. There has also been widespread international criticism.

The prisoners at Guantanamo Bay were all Muslims, but they came from many different countries. Some, for example, were British Muslims who claimed to have been in the combat zone only because they were visiting relatives in either Afghanistan or Pakistan. Countries such as Great Britain objected that the detention of their citizens was unlawful. The prisoners had not been soldiers in a regular war, and they had not been put on trial. Lawyers in the United States made the same arguments.

A prisoner is led into the cell area in Guantanamo Bay by US military personnel.

Forceful Tactics

It also became apparent that US forces were using forceful techniques to get prisoners to reveal information. One method was called waterboarding. In this, the prisoner had a cloth or towel wrapped around his head and was laid on a board with his head pointing downward. Water was poured over the cloth, so the person felt as though he were drowning. U.S. forces argued that this was necessary to force prisoners to reveal information. However, it was widely criticized as a form of torture. Torture is illegal under international law and the US Constitution.

32

TREATMENT OF TERRORISTS

WHAT'S THEIR VIEWPOINT?

In 2015, then-president Barack Obama appointed Lee Wolosky as a US special envoy [government representative] for the closure of Guantanamo Bay. Special envoys represent the US government to achieve a particular purpose. Wolosky observed that Guantanamo Bay improved over time: "It is a facility that is better than any state or local correctional facility or prison that I've been to. It's better than many of the federal facilities." However, Wolosky still believed the camp needed to be closed. He argued, "It is a recruiting tool. It is because of what the world believes that it is. It doesn't matter what it actually is in certain respects .... [It] has proven to be a recruiting tool for Islamic State." Ultimately, Wolosky failed to get Congress to agree to close the camp.

There were also reports about torture at Guantanamo Bay. The Red Cross said prisoners were kept in solitary confinement [held without contact with any other people], exposed to loud music, and beaten. After U.S. forces invaded Iraq in 2003, photographs showed U.S. personnel treating prisoners badly in Abu Ghraib, a prison near Baghdad. The damage done to the US international reputation was huge.

Denial of Rights

The authorities said these techniques were needed to gather information. For example, they used them to gain vital intelligence from Khalid Sheik Mohammed in 2007. He was a planner of the 9/11 attacks. However, critics argued that most people who were detained had no such value. Many of them were simply in the wrong place at the wrong time.

Protesters outside the White House call for the closure of the camp at Guantanamo Bay.

33

TERRORISM

The Future of Guantanamo Bay

When Barack Obama became US president in 2009, he promised to close down the prison camp at Guantanamo Bay. He said the existence of a camp outside the reach of US laws called into question the United States' reputation as a leader of civil rights. However, when Obama left office at the start of 2017, the camp was still open. The US Congress had defeated Obama's attempts to close it. Members of Congress from both political parties believed the base was necessary to keep the United States safe. However, the number of people kept in the camp fell from about 245 to 41. The released prisoners were sent back to their own countries.

As soon as he became president, Donald Trump signed an executive order keeping Guantanamo Bay open. He argued that the only way to deal with terrorists was to detain them. During his State of the Union address in January 2018, he said that any move to close the camp would be a sign of softness in the war against terrorists. Trump said, "I am also asking the Congress to ensure that, in the fight against ISIS and al-Qaeda, we continue to have all necessary power to detain terrorists—wherever we chase them down, wherever we find them—and in many cases it will now be Guantanamo Bay." In May 2018, Trump ordered the first prisoner of his presidency to be transferred to the camp.

Many politicians in Congress support keeping Guantanamo Bay open as a place to send suspected terrorists.

34

TREATMENT OF TERRORISTS

✓ PUT THE PRISONERS ON TRIAL OR LET THEM GO

Omar Deghayes is a lawyer from Chechnya who was seized by US forces in Pakistan in 2002. He spent five years at Guantanamo Bay. In 2013, he gave the prisoners' view. He said that what the prisoners wanted was an end to being detained without trial. They wanted a trial so that those who were found guilty could be imprisoned, while those who were not could be released.

✗ THE PRISONERS' DETENTION IS FAIR

Marine Corps General John Kelly commanded Guantanamo Bay from 2012 until 2016. He said when he retired that the facilities at Guantanamo Bay were decent for detainees. He asserted that every detainee was a "bad guy" although it was possible to "quibble" over exactly what they were doing on the battlefield when they were captured. In 2017, Kelly became chief of staff to President Donald Trump.

WHAT'S YOUR VIEWPOINT?

Deghayes says that prisoners should be tried to see who is guilty, but Kelly says they are all bad guys. Use these prompts to decide what you think.

- Deghayes calls for prisoners to be tried in proper courts. If prisoners were captured on a battlefield, are they still entitled to civilian trials?
- Kelly says conditions at Guantanamo Bay are good. Does that make a difference to the question of whether the detainees should be there?
- Kelly admits that some of the detainees may not have been fighting on the battlefield. In that case, how can we know if they are "bad guys"?

A demonstrator makes her feelings clear about Guantanamo Bay.

TERRORISM

CHAPTER SIX
DOMESTIC TERRORISM

Islamist terrorism sometimes appears to be the main threat to the United States, thanks to major attacks such as 9/11. However, many experts believe the country faces more of a threat from domestic terrorism—terrorist acts carried out by Americans against Americans within the United States. The definition also includes attacks by Muslims living in the United States who are motivated by radical views.

It is sometimes difficult to tell the difference between domestic terrorist attacks and other crimes or incidents of mass murder. Terrorist attacks are usually carried out either in support of or against a particular cause. They are designed either to influence government policies or to terrify the public into changing their behavior. In February 2018, for example, a gunman killed 17 people and wounded 17 more in an attack in Marjory Stoneman Douglas High School in Parkland, Florida. This was not classed as a terrorist attack though, because the gunman had no clear motives. In June 2015, however, when a gunman killed nine people in an African Methodist Episcopal Church in Mobile, South Carolina, it was clearly a terrorist attack. The attacker, Dylann Roof, was a white supremacist who had racist views of black people. Roof gave himself up the next day. He said he had wanted to begin a race war in the United States.

Dylann Roof killed nine African Americans in an attack on a prayer service at Emanuel Church in Charleston.

DOMESTIC TERRORISM

Militant Islamist Attacks

Some of the terrorist attacks in the United States have been carried out by American Muslims. In 2013, two Kyrgyz-American brothers planted a bomb near the finish of the Boston Marathon. It killed three spectators and injured hundreds more. In 2015, husband and wife Syed Rizwan Farook and Tashfeen Malik shot 14 people dead and wounded 24 in a gun attack on a holiday party in San Bernardino. In June 2016, a Muslim American named Omar Mateen killed 49 people and injured 58 at a nightclub in Orlando, Florida. However, there are many causes of domestic terrorism in the United States other than militant Islamism. That is one reason some people doubt whether a ban on travelers from some Muslim countries will help protect Americans from attack.

Other Causes

Other causes that have inspired terrorist attacks are varied. Some attacks have been carried out in the name of protecting life. Many Americans oppose abortion, for example, which is the medical termination of a pregnancy. A few individuals have attacked and killed physicians and other workers at clinics where abortions are carried out. Other terror attacks have been inspired by animal rights. The terrorists want to protect animals from being used in medical experiments or being raised in cruel conditions.

Mourners in Boston, Massachusetts, remember Dr. George Tiller, who was killed in 2009 by antiabortion extremists.

TERRORISM

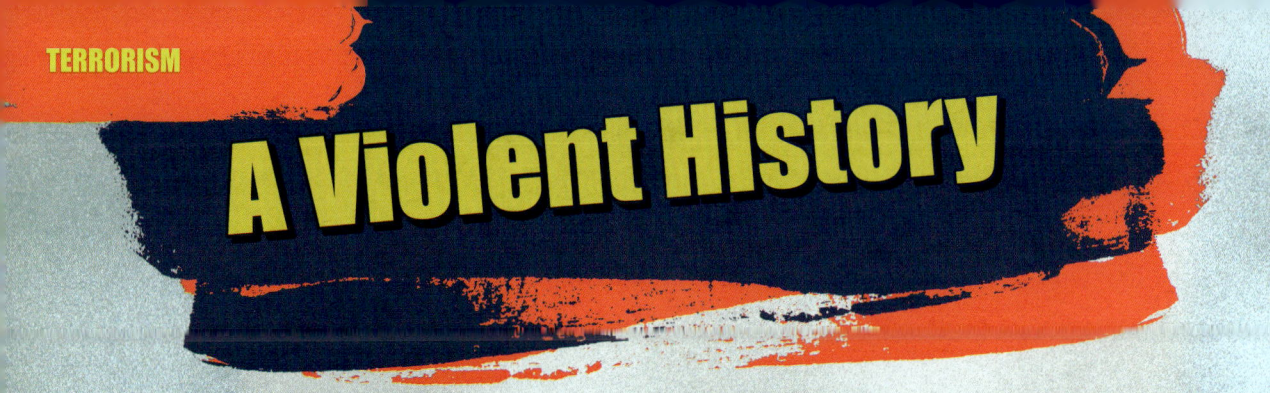

A Violent History

The United States has a long history of domestic terrorism. In the earliest days of settlement, groups of white settlers and Native Americans raided each other's communities to spread fear. Different groups of settlers also attacked one another, such as when Mormons killed about 120 settlers at Mountain Meadows in Utah in 1857.

In the early 1900s, there was a series of bomb attacks on prominent targets. In 1917, a bomb blew up at the Milwaukee Police Department, killing 10 people. In 1920, a cart loaded with dynamite blew up outside a bank on Wall Street in New York City, killing 38 people. Both attacks were believed to have been carried out by anarchists. Anarchists reject the authority of the law, because they believe people should control their own lives.

The Unabomber

One of the most infamous domestic terrorists was the Unabomber. Between 1978 and 1995, this unknown terrorist sent letter bombs to people involved in developing computers and new technology. When he was arrested in 1996, he was revealed to be a former math professor named Theodore (Ted) Kaczynski.

Mormons attacked settlers to try to deter other people from settling in Utah in the Mountain Meadows Massacre of 1857.

DOMESTIC TERRORISM

Later in the 1900s, race and religion were common motives for terror attacks. A group called the Jewish Defense League (JDL), for example, planned attacks on Arab Americans in the early 1980s. The biggest act of domestic terrorism came in 1995. A truck bomb blew up a federal building in Oklahoma City, Oklahoma, on April 19. The attack was carried out by Timothy McVeigh and Terry Nichols. They were motivated by their hatred of the US government. They believed the government had unlawfully prevented Americans from living as they chose.

This photograph shows one of the homemade bombs the Unabomber mailed to people whose views he disagreed with.

A Controversial New Law

In response to the Oklahoma City attack, Congress passed the Antiterrorism and Effective Death Penalty Act in 1996. The act was designed to make it easier for law enforcement agencies to identify suspected terrorists and charge them with crimes. It was controversial because it allowed law enforcement agencies to suspend *habeas corpus*. These are laws that limit how long the authorities can hold prisoners in detention. The law is seen as a key guarantee of individual freedom under the law.

WHAT'S THEIR VIEWPOINT?

Daryl Johnson was a senior analyst at the Department of Homeland Security before becoming a security consultant. In February 2017, after an ISIS supporter had been arrested in Missouri, he noted that the FBI was monitoring four times more cases involving Islamist extremists in the United States than domestic terrorists. Johnson told the *Kansas City Star* that he wished the FBI paid as much attention to neo-Nazis and Ku Klux Klan (KKK) members and their social media sites as they were paying to ISIS supporters. He said there were more white supremacists than ISIS supporters in the country.

The Incel Movement

One of the major recent sources of terrorist attacks in the United States has been the incel movement. These so-called involuntary celibates are young men who feel that they cannot have relationships with young women. They feel left out of society, so they become angry toward what they see as regular people, particularly women.

These flowers remember victims of an incel attack in Toronto, Canada, in April 2018 that killed 10 people.

In May 2014, a young man named Elliot Rodger killed six people and wounded many others in Isla Vista, California. The attack brought incels to public attention. Further attacks followed in Roseburg, Oregon, in 2015 and Aztec, New Mexico, in December 2017. There have also been incel attacks in Canada. The attacks were linked by misogyny, or a hatred of women. Many observers believe misogynist organizations are becoming more of a threat to US society.

The rise of incels illustrates some of the challenges involved in preventing domestic terrorism. Like radical Muslim groups, incels communicate via the Internet. They set up communities in which their ideas are not questioned. They feed off each other's anger and rage against the world. Unlike a traditional terrorist movement, however, they do not have a specific aim. No one can force women to date particular individuals. And yet the incels share a rage against the world that they believe justifies random terrorist attacks.

DOMESTIC TERRORISM

✓ SPREAD THE FOCUS MORE WIDELY

In 2017, Oren Segal, director of the Anti-Defamation League's Center on Extremism, said that programs that aim to combat violent beliefs need to focus on all the possible threats, whether they come from ISIS or the far right. Segal says that the extreme and hate-filled ideas held by extremists are spread on the Internet.

✗ FOCUS ON ISLAMIST EXTREMISTS

Brian Levin is the director of the Center for the Study of Hate and Extremism at California State University. He wrote in 2017 that militant Islamists were by no means the only current terrorist threat. He said that in the "vineyard of extremism" there were many different plants, but perhaps the greatest number of plants belonged to militant Islamism.

WHAT'S YOUR VIEWPOINT?

Segal believes there are many threats, but Levin says Islamists are the main threat. Use these prompts to figure out your viewpoint.

- Oren Segal sees all terrorists as part of the same problem. Do you think he is right to do so?
- Levin agrees that all threats must be dealt with. If there are more militant Islamists than other terrorists, would it make sense to make them the priority?
- Many experts agree with Segal that online radicalization is a danger. Why might it be such a serious threat?

Terrorism is on the decline—but is there any way it can be ended for good?

STOP TERRORISM

41

TERRORISM

Terrorism: What's Next?

What sort of terrorist attacks we face in the future, what their sources are, and how we best deal with them are complex questions. However, there are some key developments that will almost certainly play a role.

1 PREVENTING THE ATTACKS

Experts on terrorism expect more attacks to come from individuals who may be inspired by terrorist groups, but who plan and carry out their attacks themselves. Statistics suggest that these attacks usually cause fewer casualties, so they do not represent as much of a threat as large-scale attacks. Many have already been identified and halted by intelligence agencies. Major cities and tourist sites around the world have also put increased security measures in place. Armed police guard key locations, for example. Barriers have been erected to protect pedestrians from cars or trucks being driven by terrorists.

Flowers mark the site of an attack in London where a terrorist in a rental car deliberately rammed pedestrians on a bridge.

2 HUMAN RIGHTS

President Trump's decision to keep the Guantanamo Bay detention camp open will mean controversy continues about the legal status of the prisoners held there. The story has largely disappeared from the media, but 41 people remain detained. Many Americans are still uneasy about the fact that the prisoners have not been put on trial. In addition, it remains to be seen what impact the decision will have on the international reputation of the United States. The country has always been seen as a world leader on human rights, but that reputation might be damaged.

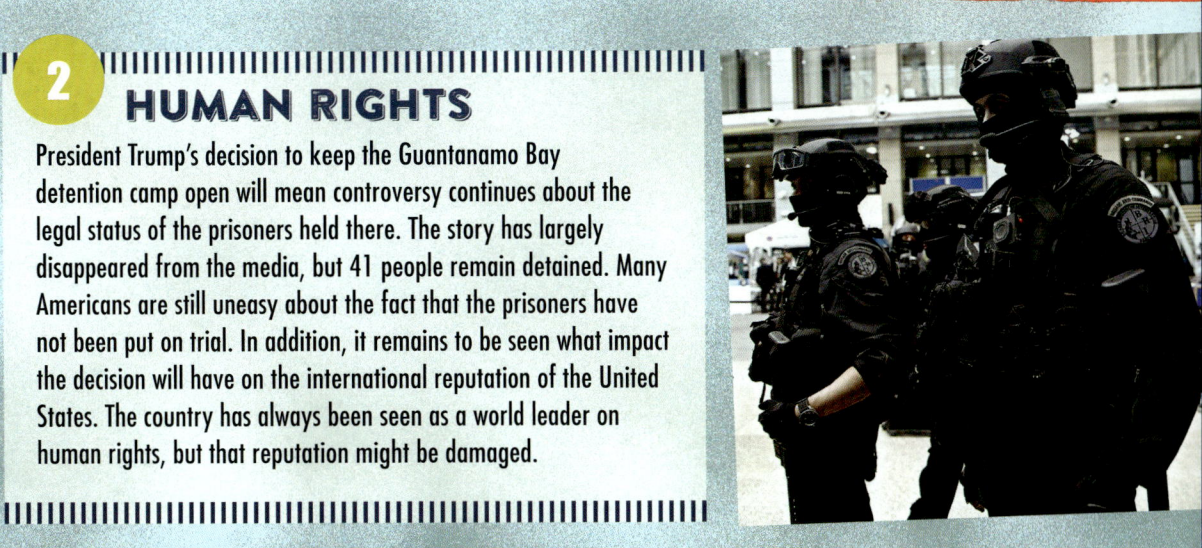

3 CHANGE IN THE MIDDLE EAST

The number of terrorist attacks in the world is falling. This is partly because the main organizations that plan major terrorist attacks are being defeated. Al-Qaeda and ISIS have suffered major setbacks in fighting against US and other forces in Afghanistan, Syria, and elsewhere. These battlefield defeats disrupt the central command of the terrorist groups, and make it harder for them to plan attacks.

4 GATHERING INTELLIGENCE

Experts agree that the ability to prevent terrorist attacks relies on gathering information. This information comes from surveillance of suspected terrorists within the United States and from an exchange of information with intelligence agencies in the countries where much terrorism begins. However, security agencies are worried that they do not have enough power to monitor possible terrorists at home. This is largely because of public concerns about government invasions of privacy. In addition, intelligence experts worry that the debate about the ban on travelers from Muslim countries will lead to less cooperation from Muslim intelligence agencies, and therefore less warning of international plots.

TERRORISM

The Future: What's Your Viewpoint?

Some observers are worried about the future of terrorism and counterterrorism. Others are more hopeful. These expert viewpoints all predict possible developments linked to subjects in this book. After reading this book, who do you think is right?

WHAT'S THEIR VIEWPOINT?

John Kerry was US Secretary of State from 2013 to 2017. After leaving office, he gave an interview to *Time* magazine. A militant Islamist suicide bomber had just killed 22 people in an attack in Manchester, England. Kerry explained why he was hopeful about the future despite such attacks. He believed that the future lay in cooperation between governments across the world, as no one government was fast enough or informed enough to act independently. He said there would always be a new terrorist group on the rise, so governments needed to have a long-term plan.

WHAT'S THEIR VIEWPOINT?

In February 2018, psychology professor Robert L. Leahy gave some advice via the *Psychology Today* website about how Americans should view terrorism. He said he did not think that Islamic State's violent and hate-filled messages would ever win. For us to win the battle against terrorism and against such ideas, we need to celebrate and support human rights, including the rights of women and gay people; democracy; free speech; and scientific truth. These ideas have more global appeal than extremist ideas.

THE FUTURE: WHAT'S YOUR VIEWPOINT?

WHAT'S THEIR VIEWPOINT?

In January 2018, Professor Stephen I. Vladeck of the University of Texas wrote an article for *CNN* about the future of Guantanamo Bay. He said that, after 17 years of military detentions in Guantanamo, we must question the rights and wrongs of long-term detentions. We must also question what the government should do with the remaining 41 detainees.

WHAT'S THEIR VIEWPOINT?

In November 2017, FBI Director Christopher Wray warned of the threat of domestic terrorism: "Domestic extremist movements collectively pose a steady threat to the United States. We anticipate [predict] law enforcement, racial minorities, and the US government will continue to be significant targets for many domestic extremist movements." These movements include white supremacists.

WHAT'S THEIR VIEWPOINT?

Matthew Heiman was a lawyer at the National Security Division of the Department of Justice. In December 2017, he noted a change in terrorist activity in the United States. In the past, al-Qaeda planned large-scale attacks that aimed at high numbers of casualties. Now, ISIS was giving its followers much less direction and training, so individuals were just grabbing cars, guns, or baseball bats.

WHAT'S YOUR VIEWPOINT?

The future of terrorism and how we fight it is complex. The viewpoints on these pages have supporters, but there are also many others. Even experts disagree about how best to stop terrorist attacks and how best to remove the causes that turn people into terrorists. Use this book as a starting point to carry out your own research in books and online to develop your own viewpoint. Remember, there is no right or wrong answer—as long as you can justify your views.

Glossary

affirm to state something publicly
allies groups or countries that work together to achieve a goal
analytic community people who analyze information
bigotry lack of tolerance toward people with other views
caliphate an area ruled by a Muslim ruler called a caliph
celibate not married or having sex
civil rights people's rights to political and social freedom and equality
colonies countries or areas under the control of other countries
combat zone the front line facing the enemy on a battlefield
controversial leading to disagreement
convicted found guilty of a crime
correctional facility a place where criminals are punished
counterterrorism measures taken to prevent terrorist attacks
detainees people held in custody
discriminated treated unfairly
domestic happening inside a country
eavesdropping secretly listening to private conversations
executive order a presidential decision that has the power of a law
extremists people with extreme political or religious views who support violent or illegal acts
hostages people captured and held to try to force something to happen
immigration coming to live permanently in another country
impacted affected by
independence freedom from being governed by another country
indiscriminate random
intelligence agencies government departments that collect military or political information
involuntary done unwillingly

Islamic related to the Muslim religion
jihadist a militant Islamist who believes he or she is fighting a holy war
liberation freedom from foreign control
militant Islamist someone who follows a very strict interpretation of Islamic laws and is prepared to use violence to see those laws put in practice
morally according to principles of right and wrong behavior
motivation someone's reason for doing something
neo-Nazis people with extreme beliefs based on those of the Nazis in Germany in the 1930s and 1940s
orchestrated organized
prohibited banned
propaganda information that is spread to support or discredit a point of view
radical extreme
recruiting persuading people to join a group
refugees people fleeing danger
resent to feel bitter about
right wing disliking liberal thought and change
sponsors people who back something
state terrorism terrorist acts carried out by governments
statistically in terms of numbers
suicide bombers terrorists who blow up bombs to kill themselves and others
surveillance close observation
think tank experts who provide advice
traitor someone who betrays their country
unconstitutional forbidden by the US Constitution
violates breaks a rule or rules
visas official permissions to stay in a country for a set length of time
white supremacist someone who believes white people are superior to people of color

For More Information

BOOKS

Kennon, Caroline. *Battling Terrorism in the United States* (American History). New York, NY: Lucent Books, 2017.

Rice, Earle, Jr. *Islamic State* (Terror Inc.). Hallendale, FL: Mitchell Lane Publishers, 2017.

Stefoff, Rebecca. *Patriot Act* (Landmark Legislation). New York, NY: Benchmark Books, 2010.

Young-Brown, Fiona. *Edward Snowden: NSA Contractor and Whistle-Blower* (Hero or Villain? Claims and Counterclaims). New York, NY: Cavendish Square, 2018.

WEBSITES

9/11 Attacks *www.ducksters.com/history/us_1900s/september_11_attacks.php*
A page about the terrorist attacks on the United States on 9/11, 2001.

Terrorism Data *ourworldindata.org/terrorism*
Details of terrorist attacks in charts and graphs.

Timeline *prospect.org/a-timeline-of-domestic-terrorism#.W6ik7y-ZOEI*
A timeline of domestic terrorism in the United States.

Travel Advice *travel.state.gov/content/travel/en/international-travel/emergencies/terrorism.html*
State Department advice for US travelers on avoiding terrorist attacks.

Publisher's note to educators and parents: Our editors have carefully reviewed these websites to ensure that they are suitable for students. Many websites change frequently, however, and we cannot guarantee that a site's future contents will continue to meet our high standards of quality and educational value. Be advised that students should be closely supervised whenever they access the Internet.

Index

9/11 attacks 6, 7, 9, 21, 22, 24–25, 30, 33, 36

abortion rights protests 37
Afghanistan 12, 16, 25, 31, 32, 43
African Methodist Episcopal Church attack 36
Ahmad, Hazrat Mirza Masroor 17
al-Baghdadi, Abu Bakr 17
al-Qaeda 9, 24, 25, 34, 43, 45
American Muslims 7, 13, 18, 25, 36, 37
animal rights protests 37
Antiterrorism and Effective Death Penalty Act 39

bin Laden, Osama 24, 25
bombings 4, 6, 9, 13, 14, 17, 24, 37, 38, 39, 44
Boston Marathon 37

Central Intelligence Agency (CIA) 24–25
counterterrorism 9, 29, 44

domestic terrorism 4, 5, 7, 8, 18, 21, 22, 24, 36–37, 40–41, 45

extremists 5, 7, 9, 13, 14, 16, 37, 39, 41, 45

Farook, Syed Rizwan 19, 37
Federal Bureau of Investigation (FBI) 24–25, 39
Florida nightclub attack 37

Guantanamo Bay 31, 32–35, 43, 45

homegrown terrorism 7, 18, 21

immigration ban 19, 20–21
incels 7, 40
intelligence agencies 5, 9, 19, 20, 23, 24–25, 26, 29, 30, 33, 42, 43
international terrorism 4, 7, 12, 15, 20, 25, 36, 43
Irish Republican Army (IRA) 8, 11
Islamist extremists 5, 7, 9, 12, 13, 14, 17
Islamic State in Iraq and Syria (ISIS) 12, 13, 17, 34, 43
Isla Vista attack 40

Jewish Defense League (JDL) 39
jihad and jihadists 15, 21, 23, 41
Johnson, Daryl 39

Kaczynski, Theodore 38

Malik, Tashfeen 19, 37
Marjory Stoneman Douglas High School attack 36
Mateen, Omar 37
McVeigh, Timothy 8, 39
Middle East 7, 8, 9, 10, 12, 13, 15, 22, 43
Mohammed, Khalid Sheik 33
Mountain Meadows Massacre 38
Munich Olympics attack 8
Muslims 7, 13, 19, 20–23

Nichols, Terry 39
Northern Ireland 8, 11
National Security Agency (NSA) 26–27, 29
Obama, Barack 12, 33, 34
Oklahoma City bombing 8, 9, 39

Pakistan 12, 16, 19, 24, 32, 35
Palestinian Liberation Organization (PLO) 8
Patriot Act 25, 26, 29

Roof, Dylann 36

San Bernardino attack 18, 19, 37
Snowden, Edward 27
suicide bombers 14, 17
surveillance 28–29
Syria 12, 16, 19, 43

Taliban 12
Tiller, Dr. George 37
Toronto attack 40
torture 32–33
Trump, President Donald 19, 21, 23, 34, 35, 43
Tunisia attack 11
Twin Towers attack 7, 9

Unabomber 38
United Kingdom 14, 42
US Constitution 19, 26
USS *Cole* 24

waterboarding 32
Weathermen 8
Wikileaks 27
Wolosky, Lee 33
World Trade Center 7, 9, 24
Wray, Christopher 45

Yousafzai, Malala 12